TABLE OF CONTENTS

CHAPTER 1

D-TOWN PROUD

The fans rise to their feet. The Dallas Mavericks are facing the Denver Nuggets. The fourth quarter is nearly over. Only 2.8 seconds remain. The score is tied 105–105. But Dallas has one more chance.

The Dallas Mavericks faced the Denver Nuggets on March 17, 2024.

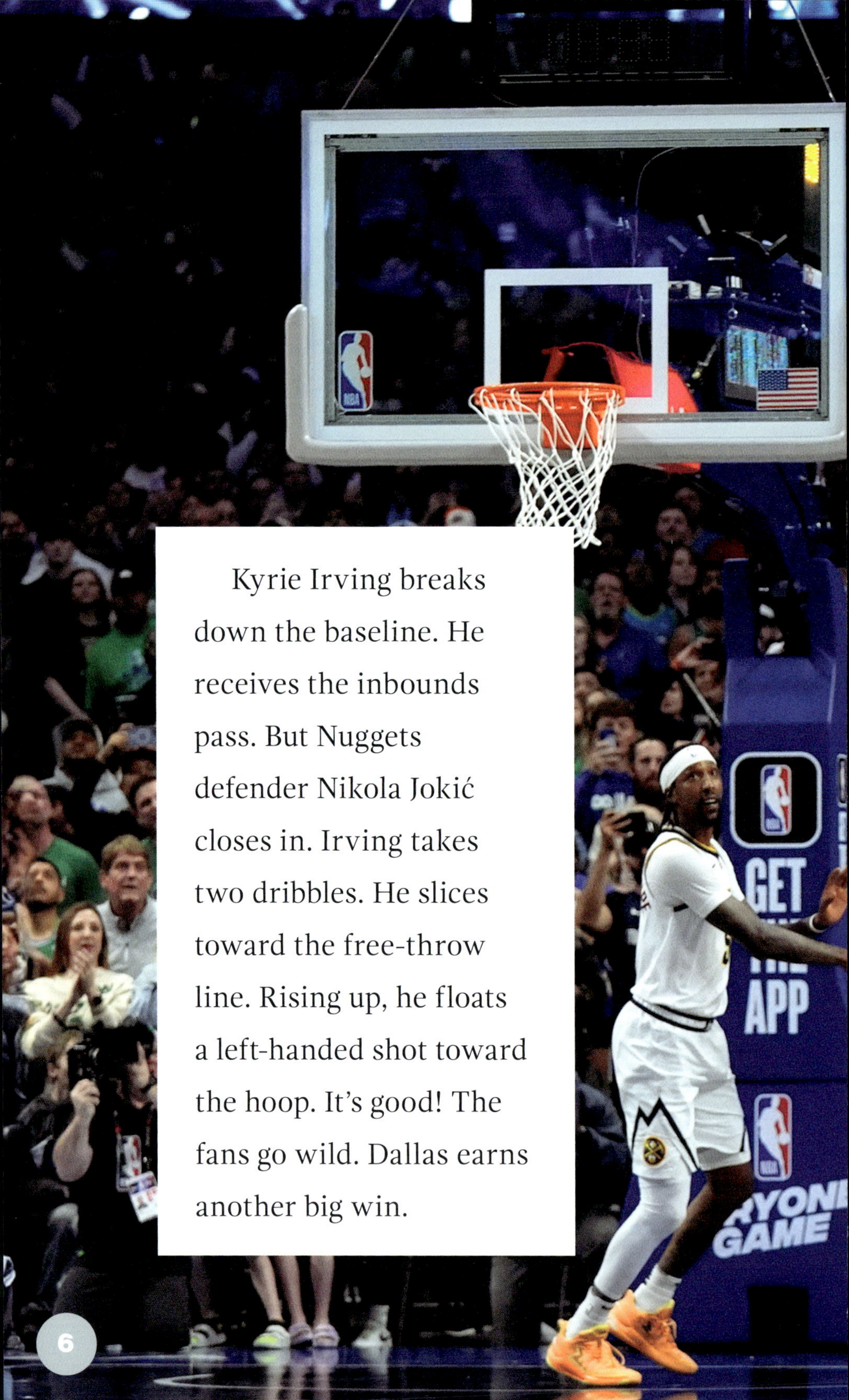

Kyrie Irving breaks down the baseline. He receives the inbounds pass. But Nuggets defender Nikola Jokić closes in. Irving takes two dribbles. He slices toward the free-throw line. Rising up, he floats a left-handed shot toward the hoop. It's good! The fans go wild. Dallas earns another big win.

Kyrie Irving (11) shoots the winning basket in a 2024 game against the Denver Nuggets.

LET'S GO

Mavs games begin with "Eminence Front." It's a rock song by The Who. A local musician known as GuitarSlayer often plays it live.

CHAPTER 2

EARLY HISTORY

In the 1960s, the Dallas Cowboys football team became successful. So, Dallas was known as a football town. Businessman Norm Sonju had other ideas. He tried to move an NBA team there in 1978. It was unsuccessful. But in 1980, he got his wish. The NBA awarded Dallas an expansion team.

Tom LaGarde attempts a shot during the Dallas Mavericks' first season.

People in Dallas were excited about the team. The Mavericks even had a new arena. But new teams usually don't have much talent. That was true for Dallas. The Mavs went 15–67 in 1980–81. It was the NBA's worst record. Still, lots of fans showed up. The future looked bright.

MAVERICKS

Fans got to vote on a team name. They selected Mavericks. It was a nod to the TV show *Maverick*. The show was a western. It aired in the 1950s and 1960s. A maverick is an independent-minded person.

Mavericks point guard Brad Davis dribbles past a defender during the 1980–81 season.

Mavericks center James Donaldson throws down a dunk during a 1988 playoff game.

Dallas began adding more skilled players. Many came from the draft. Before long, the Mavs had a winning team. From 1984 to 1990, they missed the playoffs just once. The high point came in 1988. The Mavs came within one win of the NBA Finals. However, they lost to the Los Angeles Lakers in Game 7 of the conference finals.

MILESTONE SEASON

In 1983–84, Mark Aguirre became the Mavs' first All-Star. The team went on to post Dallas's first winning record. Then the Mavs won their first playoff series.

The Mavericks struggled in the 1990s. Dallas became one of the NBA's worst teams. The 1992–93 squad lost 71 games. That was two losses shy of the NBA record. In the 1990s, the Mavs never had a winning record. However, better times were coming.

FIRST HOME

Reunion Arena opened in 1980. The Mavericks played there until 2001. For many years, the Dallas Stars hockey team shared the downtown arena. It was torn down in 2009.

Jim Jackson averaged 19.6 points per game during his five years with the Mavericks.

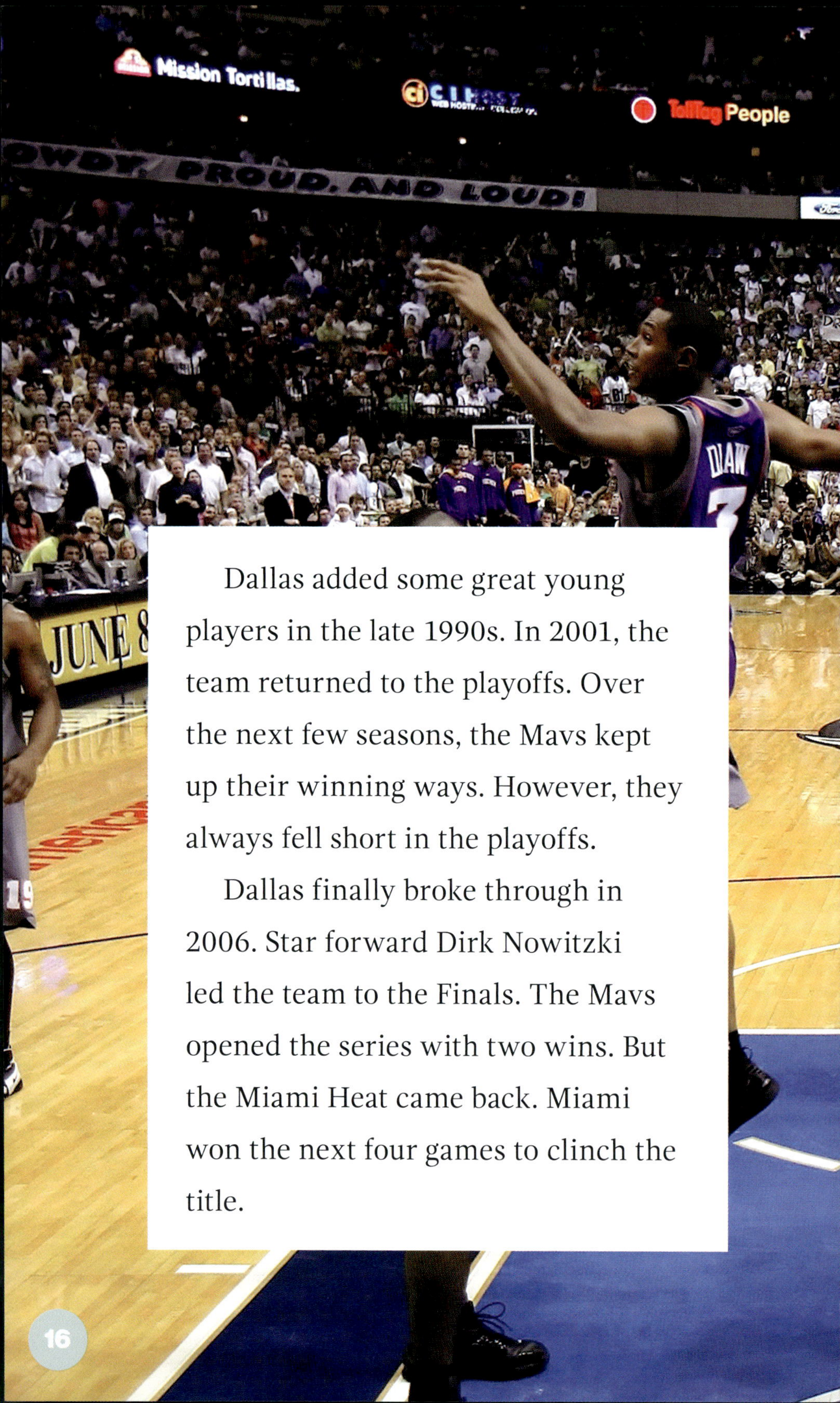

Dallas added some great young players in the late 1990s. In 2001, the team returned to the playoffs. Over the next few seasons, the Mavs kept up their winning ways. However, they always fell short in the playoffs.

Dallas finally broke through in 2006. Star forward Dirk Nowitzki led the team to the Finals. The Mavs opened the series with two wins. But the Miami Heat came back. Miami won the next four games to clinch the title.

Dirk Nowitzki (41) put up 50 points in Game 5 of the 2006 Western Conference finals.

PLAYER SPOTLIGHT

ROLANDO BLACKMAN

Rolando Blackman was born in Panama. Dallas drafted him in 1981. The guard became one of the NBA's best shooters. Over 11 seasons, he made four All-Star Games. He also led the Mavs to the playoffs six times.

BLACKMAN SCORED 16,643 POINTS IN HIS 11 SEASONS WITH THE MAVERICKS.

Eventually, the Mavs wanted a younger team. They traded Blackman in 1992. By then, he held several team records. His career scoring mark stood for 18 years. The Mavs honored Blackman in 2000. The team retired his No. 22 jersey.

DALLAS
22

CHAPTER 3

LEGENDS

Dallas picked Mark Aguirre first overall in the 1981 draft. The forward was a force under the basket. Even double-teams couldn't stop him. Aguirre played seven full seasons in Dallas. He led the team in scoring each time.

Mark Aguirre averaged 24.6 points per game as a member of the Mavericks.

The Mavs had a strong backcourt in the 1980s. Shooting guard Rolando Blackman was a reliable scorer. Derek Harper shined at point guard. He set team records for assists and steals. Forward Sam Perkins helped round out the team. He was a versatile defender. Perkins also had great instincts.

STICKING AROUND

Point guard Brad Davis joined the Mavericks in 1980. He stuck around for 44 years. Most of that time, he was a broadcaster. He also worked as an assistant coach.

Derek Harper recorded 5,111 assists in his 12 seasons with Dallas.

Jason Kidd earned Rookie of the Year honors in 1994–95. He also led the league in triple-doubles.

Three young stars brought hope to Dallas. Guard Jim Jackson and forward Jamal Mashburn were great scorers. Point guard Jason Kidd could do it all. However, the "Three J's" didn't get along. They played together from 1994 to 1996. Then the Mavs traded Kidd. Mashburn and Jackson were gone soon after.

FAMOUS OWNER

Most NBA owners stay in the background. Mark Cuban was different. The outspoken businessman owned the Mavs from 2000 to 2023. He became known for cheering loudly from his courtside seats.

Michael Finley piled up more than 12,000 points in his nine seasons with the Mavs.

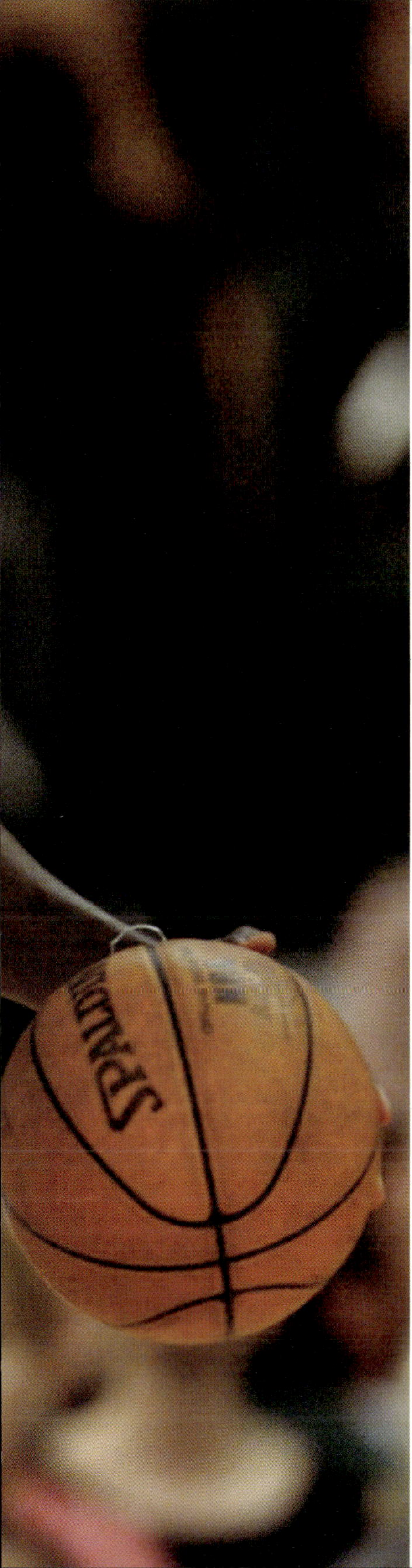

Michael Finley came to Dallas in the Kidd trade. The wing helped turn the team around. Finley was a defensive stopper. But he was best known as a shooter.

Two big helpers arrived in 1998. The Mavs traded for Steve Nash. The skilled point guard set up the offense. He could also shoot well. Rookie forward Dirk Nowitzki had a dangerous shot, too. The “Big Three” gave Dallas a top offense.

PLAYER SPOTLIGHT

DIRK NOWITZKI

Dirk Nowitzki grew up in Germany. Few in the NBA knew much about him. But the Mavericks saw potential. They traded for him on draft day in 1998. In 2019, he retired as an NBA legend.

Nowitzki stood seven feet (213 cm) tall. Yet he was an amazing shooter. His fadeaway jumper was nearly impossible to guard. Nowitzki earned Most Valuable Player (MVP) honors in 2006–07. He also led the Mavs to two NBA Finals. They won in 2011. Nowitzki was named Finals MVP.

DIRK NOWITZKI MADE THE ALL-STAR GAME 14 TIMES IN HIS 21 SEASONS.

DALLAS
41

CHAPTER 4

RECENT HISTORY

The Mavericks went 67–15 in 2006–07. That was one of the best records in NBA history. But the season ended in disaster. The Golden State Warriors upset Dallas in the first round of the playoffs.

The Mavericks became the first No. 1 seed to fall to a No. 8 seed in a seven-game playoff series.

Dallas kept making the playoffs. Even so, a championship remained out of reach. Few fans expected that to change in 2010–11. But the Mavs surprised everyone. They cruised to the Finals. The opposing Miami Heat boasted three huge stars. However, Miami had no answer for Dirk Nowitzki. The Mavs finished on a 22–5 run to win Game 2. They went on to stun the Heat in six games. At last, the Mavericks were NBA champions!

Mavericks players celebrate after winning the 2011 NBA Finals.

Soon after the Mavericks won the title, key players left the team. Dallas struggled to replace them. The Mavs missed the playoffs in 2012–13. Three first-round exits followed. Then the Mavs posted three straight losing seasons. Nowitzki retired after that. It was time to rebuild the team.

BIG WIN

One highlight came in November 2014. The Mavericks beat the Philadelphia 76ers 123–70. The 53-point win was the biggest in team history.

Wesley Matthews drives past a defender during a 2016 playoff game against the Oklahoma City Thunder.

Luka Dončić averaged 32.4 points per game in the 2024 conference finals.

By 2018–19, a new era was beginning. Teenage forward Luka Dončić won the Rookie of the Year Award. Soon, he lifted Dallas back into the playoffs. The team reached the conference finals in 2022. Two years later, the Mavs caught fire late. They made it all the way to the Finals. The thrilling run ended in a loss to the Boston Celtics.

SHOCKING TRADE

In February 2025, the Mavs traded Luka Dončić. In return, Dallas received Anthony Davis. The move stunned fans. Some said it was the most surprising trade in NBA history.

CHAPTER 5

MODERN STARS

In 2010–11, center Tyson Chandler lifted Dallas's defense. His presence under the hoop helped the Mavs win a championship. Chandler left the team after that. A few years later, he came back for one more season.

Tyson Chandler racked up 692 rebounds in the 2010–11 season.

Longtime forward Dirk Nowitzki led the way in Dallas. Some of his best seasons came alongside Jason Terry. The point guard was best known for his shooting. In the 2006 Finals, he averaged 22 points per game. In later years, he usually came off the bench. But his impact remained great. Terry helped Dallas win the title in 2011.

WELCOME BACK

In 2008, point guard Jason Kidd returned to Dallas. The future Hall of Famer played a key role in the 2011 championship. In 2021, he came back again as the Mavs' head coach.

Jason Terry celebrates after draining a three-pointer in a 2011 game against the Phoenix Suns.

The Mavs won only 33 games in 2018–19. But rookie guard Luka Dončić shined. His offensive skills set him apart. Jalen Brunson was also a rookie that year. By 2021–22, he was the starting point guard. He and Dončić formed a high-scoring backcourt. They led Dallas to the conference finals. However, Brunson left after that season.

TOP COACH

Rick Carlisle coached the Mavs from 2008 to 2021. In that time, he won 555 games. That set a team record. He also led the team to the 2011 championship.

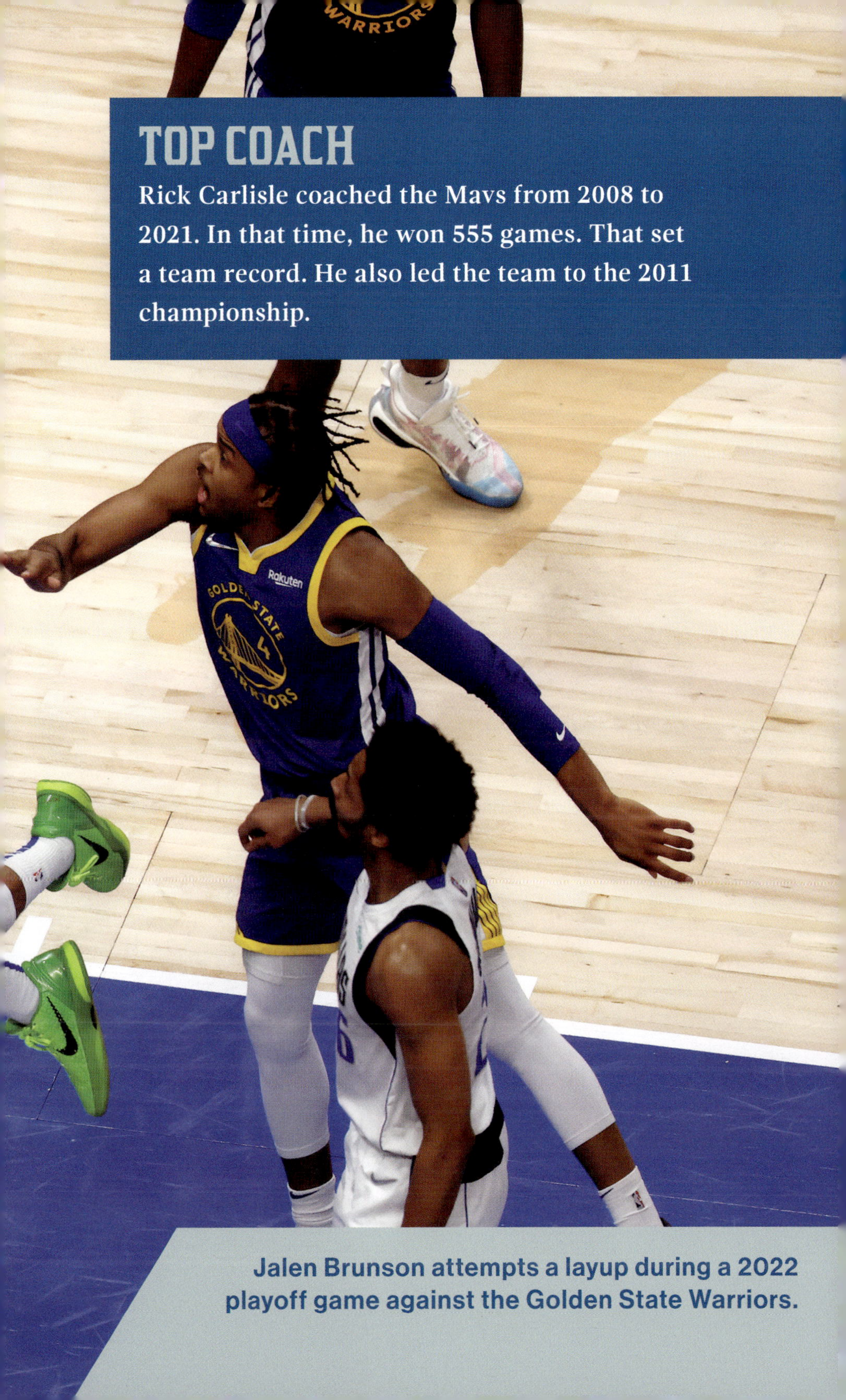

Jalen Brunson attempts a layup during a 2022 playoff game against the Golden State Warriors.

Dallas signed Kyrie Irving in 2023. The point guard thrived. He helped Dallas reach the 2024 Finals.

In 2025, Irving got a new partner. Anthony Davis was known for being dominant under the hoop. He was a great rebounder. But he could also score.

NEXT STAR

The Mavericks had the first pick in the 2025 draft. They selected Cooper Flagg. In college, Flagg had been an amazing defender. He was also great at scoring. Dallas fans hoped Flagg would become the Mavs' next star.

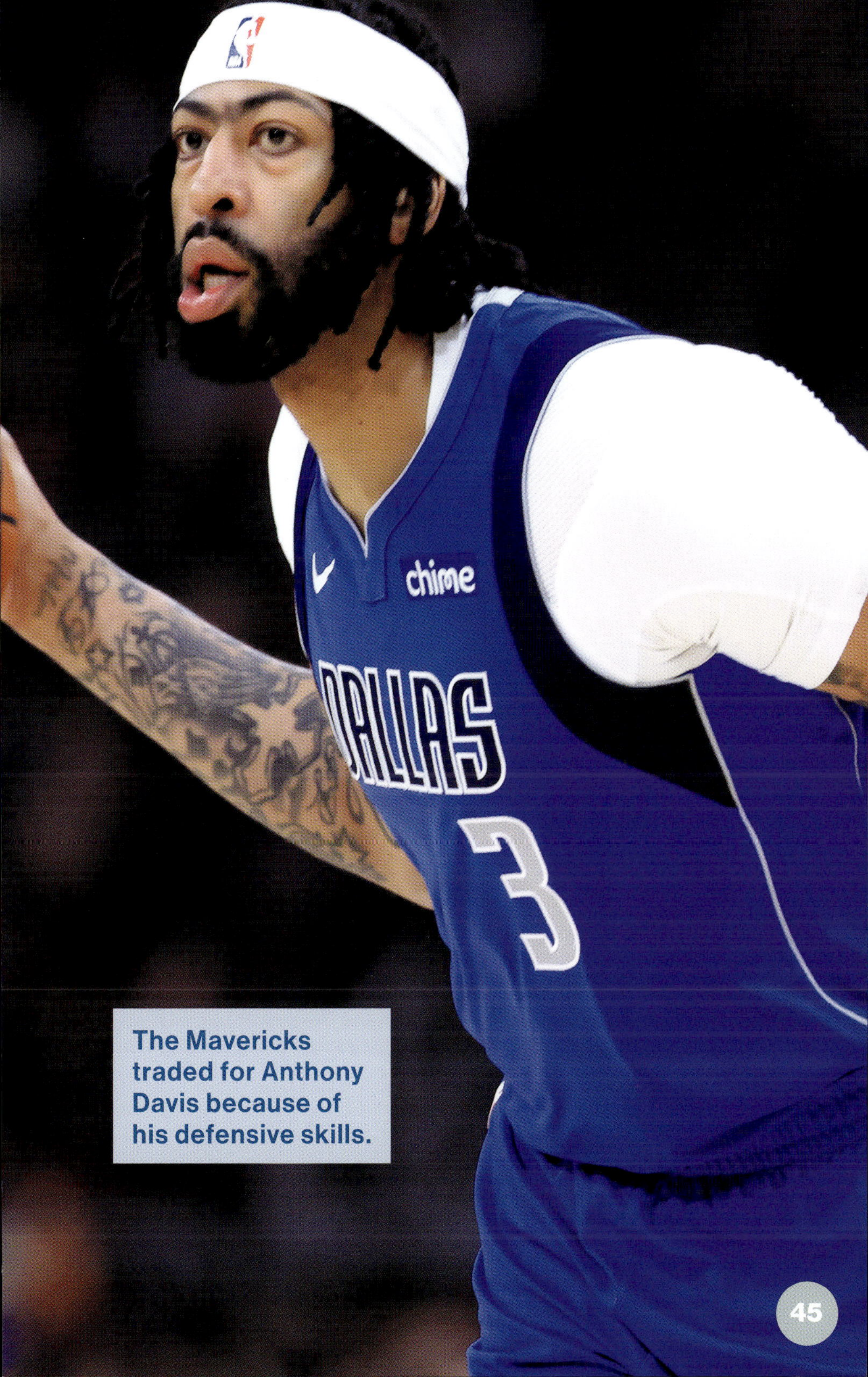

The Mavericks traded for Anthony Davis because of his defensive skills.

PLAYER SPOTLIGHT

LUKA DONČIĆ

Luka Dončić grew up in Slovenia. By age 16, he was playing for Real Madrid. That's one of Spain's top pro teams. By age 19, Dončić was ready for the NBA. The guard arrived in Dallas in 2018. He was a star from the start.

Dončić piled up points. No one could guard his step-back jumper. He also dazzled with flashy passes. Fans were amazed by his court vision. Dončić racked up many triple-doubles. And in 2024, he led Dallas all the way to the Finals.

IN 2023–24, LUKA DONČIĆ LED THE NBA WITH AN AVERAGE OF 33.9 POINTS PER GAME.

chime
MAVS
77
Wilson

CHAPTER 6

TEAM TRIVIA

The Mavericks have two mascots. MavsMan dresses like a superhero. He first appeared in 1996. An updated MavsMan arrived in 2022. By then, Champ was also around. Champ is a blue horse with a white mane.

Champ fires up the crowd before Mavericks games.

Big changes came to Dallas in 2001. The Mavericks moved into a new arena. The Mavericks updated their look that year, too. Their original logo was blue, green, and white. It featured a cowboy hat. The current Mavs logo shows a horse. The team's colors are now blue, silver, and black.

The Mavericks' arena can hold more than 21,000 fans.

SELLOUT STREAK

The Mavericks sold out their game on December 15, 2001. After that, they didn't stop. On February 12, 2020, the Mavs sold out their 815th home game in a row. That set an NBA record. Going into the 2025–26 season, the streak was still going strong.

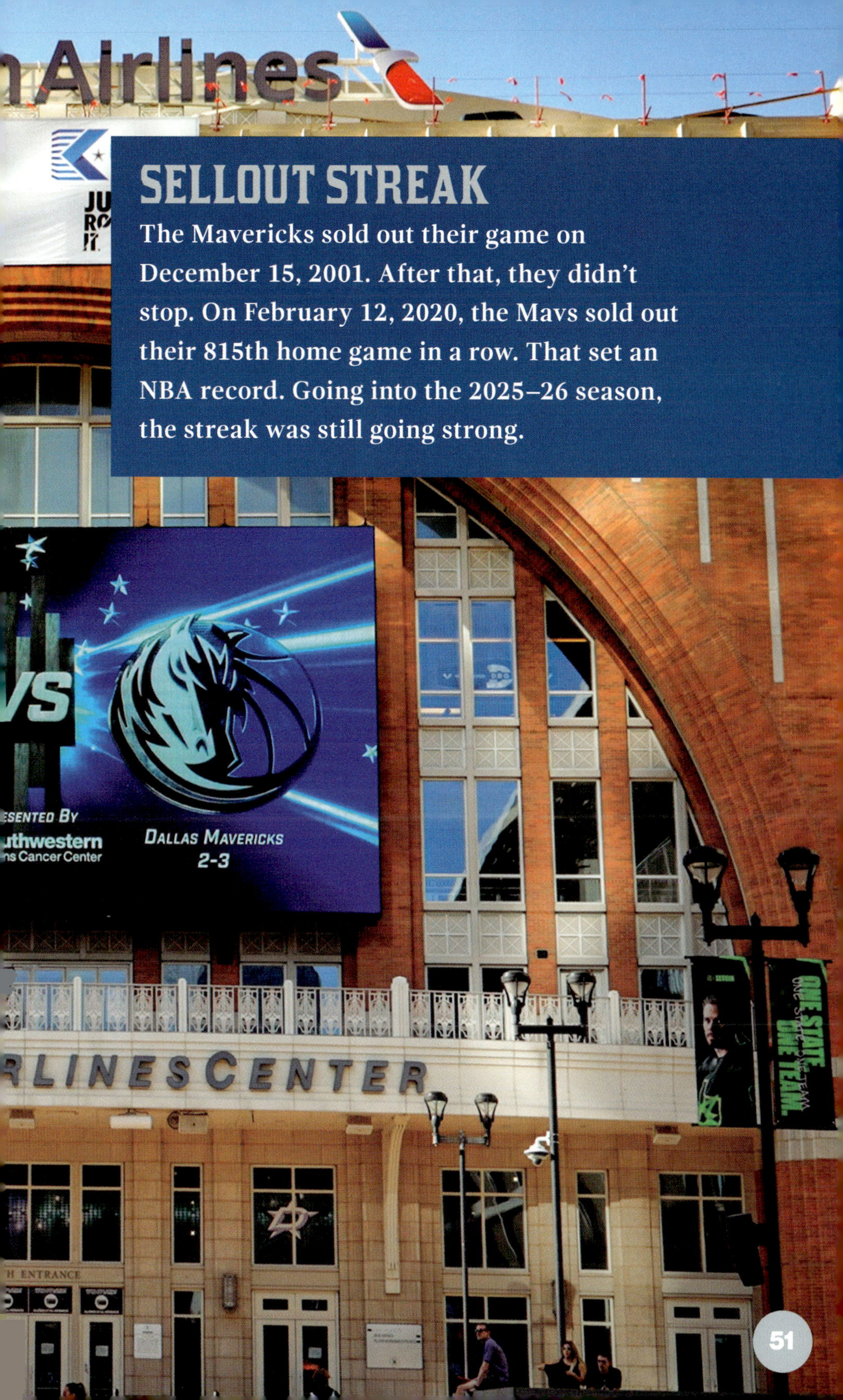

Luka Dončić scores two of his 73 points against the Atlanta Hawks on January 26, 2024.

Mavs players have enjoyed some amazing games. In 2001, Michael Finley recorded 10 steals in a single game. In a 2011 playoff game, Dirk Nowitzki went 24-for-24 from the free throw line. And in a 2024 game, Luka Dončić scored 73 points. That ranked fourth in NBA history.

STANDING TALL

Shawn Bradley stood seven feet, six inches (229 cm) tall. Only two players in NBA history were taller. In a 1998 game, Bradley blocked 13 shots. That was two shy of the NBA record.

The ABA began play in 1967. This league was separate from the NBA. One of its teams played in Dallas. The Chaparrals lasted six seasons. However, they moved to San Antonio. They became the Spurs. In the Mavericks' first NBA game, they hosted the Spurs. The teams still have a rivalry. Dallas also has a rivalry with Texas's other team, the Houston Rockets.

Mavericks forward Naji Marshall battles through two defenders during a 2024 game against the San Antonio Spurs.

TEAM RECORDS

All-Time Points: **31,560**

Dirk Nowitzki (1998–2019)

All-Time Assists: **5,111**

Derek Harper (1983–94, 1996–97)

All-Time Rebounds: **11,489**

Dirk Nowitzki (1998–2019)

All-Time Steals: **1,551**

Derek Harper (1983–94, 1996–97)

All-Time Blocks: **1,281**

Dirk Nowitzki (1998–2019)

All-Time Three-Pointers: **1,982**

Dirk Nowitzki (1998–2019)

All-Time Triple-Doubles: **80**

Luka Dončić (2018–25)

All-Time Coaching Wins: **555**

Rick Carlisle (2008–21)

NBA MVPs: **1**

Dirk Nowitzki (2006–07)

NBA Championships: **1**

2010–11

All statistics are accurate through the 2024–25 season.

DALLAS
41

TIMELINE

1980

In their first NBA game, the Mavericks beat the San Antonio Spurs 103–92.

1981

The Mavericks select Mark Aguirre first overall and Rolando Blackman ninth overall in the NBA Draft. Both become key players for the team.

1988

The Mavericks reach the Western Conference finals but lose to the Los Angeles Lakers in Game 7.

1993

The Mavericks win their last two games but still finish with 71 losses.

1998

The Mavericks trade for forward Dirk Nowitzki on draft day.

2001

The Mavericks begin their record sellout streak.

2006

The Mavericks reach the Finals but fall to the Miami Heat in six games.

2007

Nowitzki becomes the first European player to win the NBA MVP Award.

2011

Dallas beats the Miami Heat in Game 6 of the Finals. The win secures the Mavericks' first NBA title.

2024

Luka Dončić and Kyrie Irving lead the Mavs back to the Finals, but they fall to the Boston Celtics in five games.

COMPREHENSION QUESTIONS

Write your answers on a separate piece of paper.

1. Write a paragraph that explains the main ideas of Chapter 2.
2. Who do you think was the best player in Mavericks history? Why?
3. Who was the Mavericks' first All-Star?
   - A. Rolando Blackman
   - B. Mark Aguirre
   - C. Dirk Nowitzki
4. Why did people think the NBA might struggle in Dallas?
   - A. The city has fewer people than most other NBA cities.
   - B. There were not enough players to form a team in Dallas.
   - C. Football was the most popular sport in Dallas.

5. What does **clinch** mean in this book?

The Mavs opened the series with two wins. But the Miami Heat came back. Miami won the next four games to ***clinch*** *the title.*

A. to lose after being ahead
B. to stop trying during a game
C. to make something certain

6. What does **potential** mean in this book?

Few in the NBA knew much about him. But the Mavericks saw ***potential****. They traded for him on draft day in 1998. In 2019, he retired as an NBA legend.*

A. the ability to be great
B. the place where a person is born
C. the people who run a sports team

Answer key on page 64.

GLOSSARY

assists
Passes that lead directly to baskets.

backcourt
The players who usually play farther away from the basket.

broadcaster
Someone whose job involves speaking on a radio or TV show.

draft
A system that lets teams select new players coming into the league.

expansion team
A new team that is added to a league.

mascots
Figures that are the symbols of sports teams.

rivalry
An ongoing competition that brings out strong emotion from fans and players.

rookie
An athlete in his or her first year as a professional player.

triple-doubles
Games in which a player records 10 or more of three different stats.

versatile
Able to do many things well.

wing
A player who can play guard or forward.

TABLE OF CONTENTS

CHAPTER 1

Triple Threat

The ball bounces off the rim. Shoes squeak on the court. Players run to the ball. Russell Westbrook watches. He is surrounded by taller players. But no matter. Westbrook knows he can beat them.

He leaps up. He tips the ball back toward the basket. It drops through. Westbrook is 6-foot-3 (1.91 m). That is shorter than many players. But it doesn't stop him from being a star.

This April 2017 game is important. His Oklahoma City Thunder are playing the Denver Nuggets. Westbrook can break a National Basketball Association (NBA) record. It is for most **triple-doubles** in one season.

FUN FACT

The average NBA player is about 6-foot-7 (2 m)!

Russell Westbrook is not the tallest player on the court, but he brings skill and passion to his game.

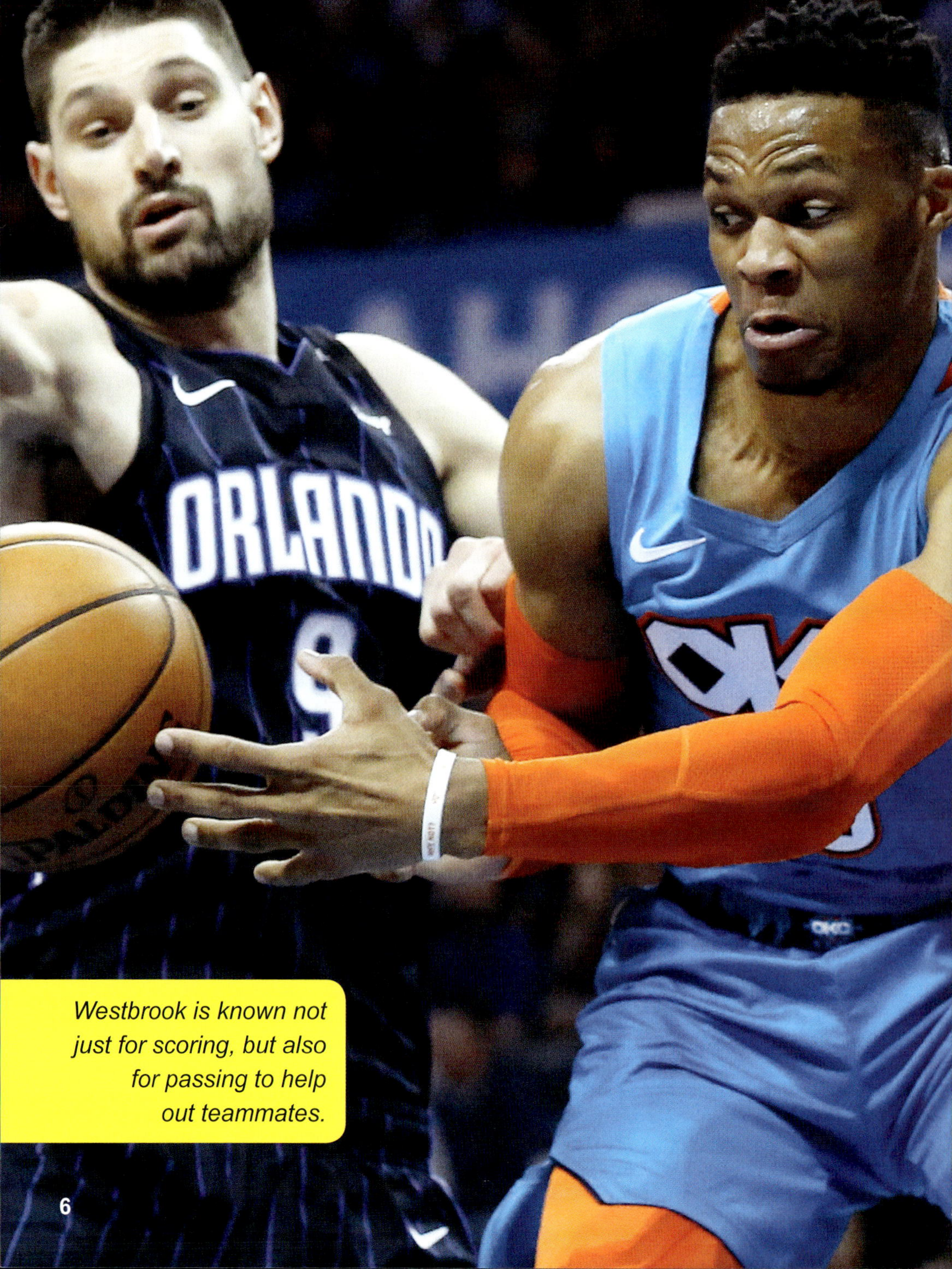

Westbrook is known not just for scoring, but also for passing to help out teammates.

Westbrook handles the ball in the second quarter. He dribbles just inside the three-point line. He fires up a shot. Westbrook starts running back. He knows it's going in. Swish! Westbrook is confident. He backs it up on the court.

Now it's the fourth quarter. Westbrook looks to the right corner. Just a few minutes remain. He sees Semaj Christon open. Westbrook fires a pass. Christon throws up a three-point shot. It's good! It is Westbrook's tenth **assist** of the game. That gives him a triple-double. It is his 42nd of the season. That is a new record.

Westbrook still has more in him. Oklahoma City trails 105–103. Only three seconds are left. Thunder teammate Steven Adams gets the ball. He passes to Westbrook. Westbrook jumps up. He launches a three-point shot. The ball rings through the hoop. The buzzer sounds! The Thunder win 106–105.

Westbrook jumps in the air. His teammates run over to celebrate. Westbrook finished the game with 50 points. He added 16 rebounds and 10 assists. Westbrook helped turn the Thunder into a great team. Doing that took a lot of hard work.

Westbrook celebrates with teammates after winning the game and setting a new record.

CAREER STATS

Through the 2018–19 season

POINTS PER GAME	23.0
REBOUNDS PER GAME	7.0
ASSISTS PER GAME	8.4
CAREER POINTS	18,859
THREE-POINT ACCURACY	30.8%

CHAPTER 2

California Dreaming

Russell Westbrook stood in the park with his dad. Russell was taking shots. He did it over and over. Then it was time to work out. He did push-ups. He did pull-ups. And he did sit-ups.

Russell was born on November 12, 1988. He grew up near Los Angeles, California. He loved basketball as a kid. He spent hours playing with his dad and friends.

Many players get their start playing on public courts with their parents or friends.

Westbrook pays tribute to his friend with a bracelet. He wears it when he arrives on the court for warm-ups and stretching.

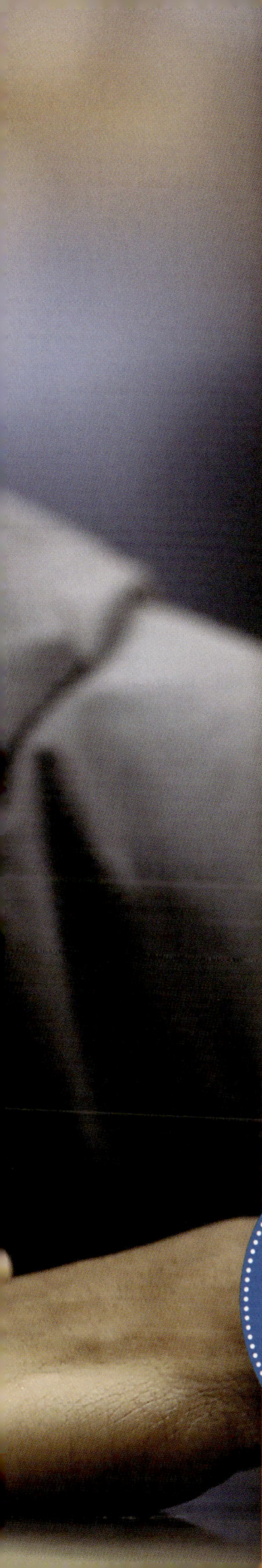

Khelcey Barrs was Russell's best friend. The two spent many hours playing basketball. They played together in **pickup** games. They wanted to play together in high school and college.

One day, Khelcey was playing pickup basketball. He fell on the floor. Players thought he was joking. But Khelcey had a heart condition. He didn't even know about it. He died at age 16. Russell still remembers his friend. He wears a bracelet that says "KB3."

College coaches didn't look at Russell right away. He was 5-foot 8 (1.73 m). He weighed 140 pounds (64 kg). But then he grew. Russell was taller and heavier. Then the University of California, Los Angeles (UCLA) saw him play. And they wanted him. UCLA was the school of Russell's dreams.

FUN FACT

Russell grew five inches (12.7 cm) between his junior and senior seasons.

Where Westbrook Has Been

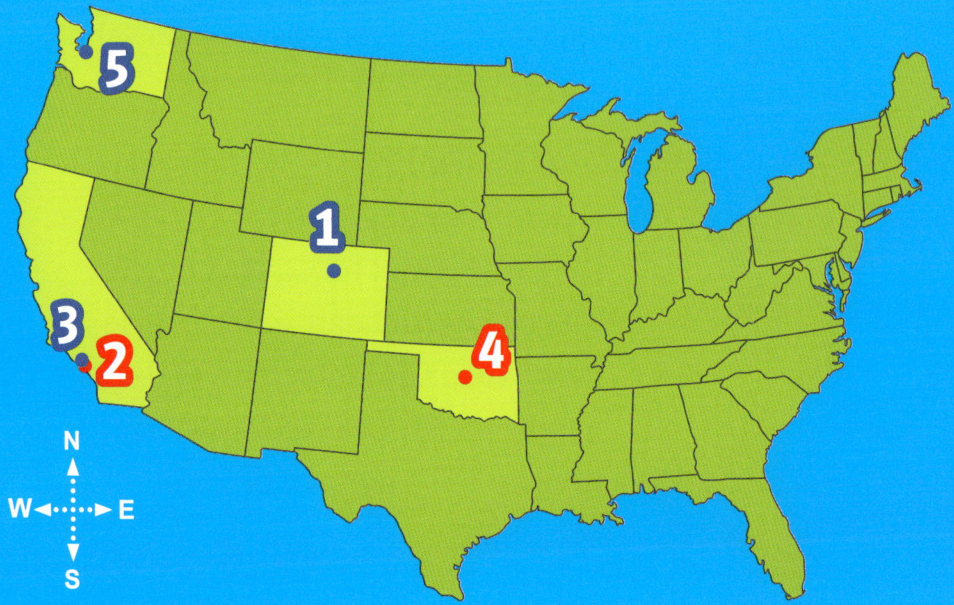

1 **Denver, Colorado:** This is the city where Westbrook set the NBA record for most triple-doubles in one season.

2 **Long Beach, California:** Westbrook was born here on November 12, 1988.

3 **Los Angeles, California:** Westbrook played here for UCLA for two seasons before going to the NBA.

4 **Oklahoma City, Oklahoma:** Westbrook's first season in Oklahoma City was during the 2008–09 season.

5 **Seattle, Washington:** Before moving to Oklahoma City, the Thunder were known as the Seattle SuperSonics. They were the SuperSonics when they drafted Westbrook in 2008.

Russell struggled during his first year there. He averaged only 3.4 points per game. But the UCLA Bruins made it to the **Final Four**.

Russell wanted to be better next year. He woke up at 6:00 a.m. every day in the summer. He worked out and practiced. He played pickup games. Sometimes NBA players like Kobe Bryant joined in.

The hard work paid off. UCLA went back to the Final Four. Russell was named a top defensive player. He decided to leave after his **sophomore** year. It was time to see what he could do in the NBA.

CHAPTER 3

A Family Man

More than 300 kids cheered Russell Westbrook. He handed out high-fives. Then he started handing out presents.

Westbrook was playing Santa. He was hosting a Christmas party for kids. He enjoys meeting Oklahoma City families who need help. During the Christmas season, he brings them clothes and other gifts. He does this as part of his **charity** work. Westbrook has his own charity. It is called the Russell Westbrook Why Not? Foundation.

In December 2017 Westbrook filled up a shopping cart full of toys for kids.

Westbrook started his charity in 2012. He works with kids who face challenges. The charity's name gets people to think about what is possible. Westbrook wants everyone to ask, "Why not?" He wants people to never give up on their dreams. Westbrook's father taught him this lesson.

FUN FACT

Westbrook has one sibling, his younger brother Reynard.

Westbrook also helped open reading centers. He wants kids to read. The NBA gave him an award in 2015 for his charity work.

Westbrook helps his charity serve Thanksgiving dinner to a Los Angeles community in 2016.

Companies hire Westbrook for **endorsements**. He has his own line of basketball shoes. Westbrook enjoys fashion. It is an interest off the court too. In 2013, he signed a deal with an underwear company. He designs custom underwear. He also worked with a fashion company to design jeans. Westbrook has appeared in soda ads too.

Westbrook lives with his wife and children. He met his wife, Nina, at UCLA. She played on the women's basketball team. They married in 2015. Westbrook's oldest child, Noah, was born in 2017. Their twin daughters were born in November 2018.

FUN FACT

The high-end store Barney's sold Westbrook's line of sunglasses.

Westbrook enjoys showing off his sense of style.

CAREER TIMELINE

1988

November 12, 1988
Russell Westbrook is born in Long Beach, California.

2007

March 31, 2007
Westbrook plays in the Final Four with UCLA as a freshman.

2008

June 26, 2008
The Seattle SuperSonics select Westbrook with the fourth pick in the NBA Draft.

2008

October 29, 2008
Westbrook makes his NBA debut with the Oklahoma City Thunder.

2012

June 12, 2012
Westbrook plays in his first NBA Finals game with the Thunder.

2017

April 9, 2017
Westbrook sets the NBA record for most triple-doubles in one season.

2017

June 26, 2017
The NBA names Westbrook the 2016–17 Most Valuable Player (MVP).

CHAPTER 4

Thunder and Lightning

Russell Westbrook came into the NBA with Kevin Durant. Together, they turned the Thunder into a great team. Durant and Westbrook played together from 2008 to 2016. Each had his own strengths. Both helped the Thunder win. The team made it to the 2012 NBA Finals.

Durant and Westbrook became successful teammates with the Thunder.

Westbrook could hit any shot. He also wowed fans with dunks. Clips of his dunks became popular online. In 2016, Oklahoma City played the Golden State Warriors in the conference finals. The Thunder went up 3–1 in the series. But the Warriors **rallied** to beat Oklahoma City.

FUN FACT

Westbrook won a gold medal with Team USA at the 2012 Olympics.

ON THE MOVE

The Seattle SuperSonics took Westbrook in the 2008 NBA Draft. He was the fourth pick. Weeks later, things changed. The team moved to Oklahoma City. They became the Thunder. The city of Seattle fought to keep its team. But the owner moved the team anyway. Westbrook played his first season with the Thunder. He never wore a SuperSonics jersey.

Westbrook finished an amazing season in 2017.

Durant became a **free agent** after that season. Many teams wanted him. He decided to go to Golden State. Westbrook stayed in Oklahoma City. He signed a new contract with the Thunder in 2016.

The NBA began in 1949. Until 2017, only one person had averaged a triple-double for a season. Westbrook became the second. He won the Most Valuable Player (MVP) award that season. He beat out other star players such as Stephen Curry and Kawhi Leonard.

Oklahoma City tried to find help for Westbrook. The team traded for Paul George. He was a star for the Indiana Pacers. Westbrook averaged a triple-double again.

FUN FACT

Oscar Robertson was the first NBA player to average a triple-double. He did it in 1962.

Westbrook had another great year in 2018–19. He was close to averaging a triple-double. It came down to the season's last day. Westbrook needed 16 rebounds. He got 20. He got his third triple-double season in a row!

He was already a great player. How great could he be? "He'll go down as a Hall of Famer," George said. "One of the best."

Westbrook continued to shine in 2019.

BEYOND THE BOOK

After reading the book, it's time to think about what you learned. Try the following exercises to jumpstart your ideas.

THINK

THAT'S NEWS TO ME. Russell Westbrook set the NBA record for triple-doubles in a season in 2017. How might news sources be able to fill in more detail about this? What new information could you find in news articles? Where could you go to find those sources?

CREATE

PRIMARY SOURCES. A primary source is an original document, photograph, or interview. Make a list of different primary sources you might be able to find about Westbrook. What new information might you learn from these sources?

SHARE

SUM IT UP. Write one paragraph summarizing the important points from this book. Make sure it's in your own words. Share the paragraph with a classmate. Does your classmate have any comments about the summary? Does he or she have additional questions about Westbrook?

GROW

REAL-LIFE RESEARCH. What places could you visit to learn more about Westbrook? What other things could you learn while you were there?

RESEARCH NINJA

Visit www.ninjaresearcher.com/0462 to learn how to take your research skills and book report writing to the next level!

RESEARCH

DIGITAL LITERACY TOOLS

SEARCH LIKE A PRO
Learn about how to use search engines to find useful websites.

FACT OR FAKE?
Discover how you can tell a trusted website from an untrustworthy resource.

TEXT DETECTIVE
Explore how to zero in on the information you need most.

SHOW YOUR WORK
Research responsibly—learn how to cite sources.

WRITE

GET TO THE POINT
Learn how to express your main ideas.

PLAN OF ATTACK
Learn prewriting exercises and create an outline.

DOWNLOADABLE REPORT FORMS

Further Resources

BOOKS

Doeden, Matt. *Russell Westbrook*. Lerner, 2017.

Kortemeier, Todd. *Russell Westbrook: Basketball Star.* Focus Readers, 2018.

Nagelhout, Ryan. *Russell Westbrook: Triple-Double Superstar*. Britannica Educational Publishing, 2019.

WEBSITES

FACTSURFER

Factsurfer.com gives you a safe, fun way to find more information.

1. Go to www.factsurfer.com.
2. Enter "Russell Westbrook" into the search box and click 🔍.
3. Select your book cover to see a list of related websites.

Glossary

assist: When a player passes to another player who then scores a basket, the first player gets an assist. Westbrook got an assist after passing to Kevin Durant.

charity: A charity is a group that helps and raises money for those in need. Westbrook's charity helps kids in Oklahoma City.

endorsements: Endorsements are when someone gives their approval to something. Westbrook does endorsements for products such as soda and clothing.

Final Four: When just four teams are left in the March Madness college basketball tournament, that stage is called the Final Four. UCLA played in the Final Four in 2007.

free agent: A free agent is someone who does not have a contract to play with a team. Kevin Durant became a free agent in 2016.

pickup: In basketball, a pickup game does not have standard officials or rules. Westbrook played a lot of pickup basketball as a kid.

rallied: When a team has overcome a deficit, they have rallied in the game or series. The Golden State Warriors rallied against the Thunder in the 2016 NBA playoffs.

sophomore: A second-year student is called a sophomore. Westbrook was an all-conference player as a sophomore.

triple-doubles: Triple-doubles are recorded when a player has 10 or more of three statistics in a game, such as points or rebounds. Westbrook has gotten triple-doubles in many games.

Index

PHOTO CREDITS

The images in this book are reproduced through the courtesy of: Brian Rothmuller/Icon Sportswire/AP Images, front cover (center), p. 9 (Russell Westbrook); Sue Ogrocki/AP Images, front cover (right), pp. 3, 6–7, 16–17; David Zalubowski/AP Images, pp. 4–5; Ververidis Vasilis/Shutterstock Images, p. 7; Jack Dempsey/AP Images, p. 8; Red Line Editorial, pp. 9 (chart), 14; Daniel Loncarevic/Shutterstock Images, pp. 10, 21 (top); asife/Shutterstock Images, pp. 10–11; Christian Petersen/Getty Images Sport/Getty Images, pp. 12–13; Photo Works/Shutterstock, p. 15; s_bukley/Shutterstock Images, p. 16; Lilly Lawrence/Getty Images Entertainment/Getty Images, pp. 18–19; Featureflash Photo Agency/Shutterstock Images, p. 20; Lightspring/Shutterstock Images, p. 21 (bottom); Jeff Roberson/AP Images, p. 22; Victor Maschek/Shutterstock Images, p. 24; David J. Phillip/AP Images, pp. 24–25; Oleksiy Naumov/Shutterstock Images, p. 26; Brandon Dill/AP Images, pp. 26–27; Cressida Studio/Shutterstock Images, p. 30.

ABOUT THE AUTHOR

Kevin Frederickson is a freelance writer and editor from Ohio. He lives near Cincinnati with his golden doodle, Max.